butter
        comes from
butterflies

when I was a kid, I used to believe...

butter

comes from

butterflies

compiled by Mat Connolley

illustrations by Scott Menchin

CHRONICLE BOOKS

SAN FRANCISCO

ISBN: *0-8118-4436-6*

Manufactured in *China*
Designed by *Vivien Lung*
Typeset in New Century Schoolbook
and Schulschrift

Distributed in Canada by Raincoast Books
9050 Shaughnessy Street
Vancouver, British Columbia V6P 6E5

10 9 8 *7* 6 5 4 3 2 *1*

Chronicle Books LLC
85 Second Street
San Francisco, California 94105
www.chroniclebooks.com

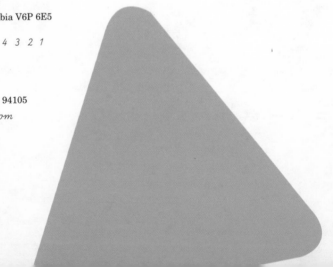

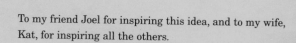

To my friend Joel for inspiring this idea, and to my wife, Kat, for inspiring all the others.

A huge thank-you to everyone who has contributed beliefs to my collection. It really would be nothing without you!

Introduction

when I was a kid,

I had a morbid fear of the toilet. I was convinced that there was a vampire living just around the S-bend who would attack me if I spent too long sitting there, so I'd always go as quickly as possible.

Many years later, after I found out that a good friend used to believe his body was filled with baked beans, I began collecting people's strange childhood beliefs. This collection evolved into a Web site, iusedtobelieve.com, which now has thousands of entries covering every topic imaginable. If you want to add your own, go to www.iusedtobelieve.com/add/ and share it with the world!

As my collection grew, it became clear that some childhood delusions are rather common, such as the belief that cats are really female dogs, that swallowing seeds will cause fruit to sprout from your ears, or that a thunderstorm is the sound of God bowling. Some of these beliefs come from overactive imaginations, but a lot are the result of parental misinformation, such as telling children that the ice-cream van only plays music when it's run out of ice cream.

This book will remind you of what it was like to be a child, fascinated and horrified by the world around you. It will also reassure you that the things you used to believe weren't so strange after all!

— *Mat Connolley*, mat@iusedtobelieve.com

When I was very young
I was convinced that a
zebra was a flightless bird.

Thom

For years I believed
that cheerleaders had
surgery to replace their
hands with pom-poms.

R.

When I was young I believed that windmills in farmers' fields were used to keep the cows **cool**.

Linda

My older brother told me that prawns came from Mars, which is how the planet got its color.

B.

I used to think that sugar-free chewing gum meant there was a special offer where you got a free bag of sugar if you sent in the wrapper. *Anonymous*

After reading the newspaper obituary column I believed that everyone died in alphabetical order, and I wished I could be called

Mr. Zebedee.

Brian

Our fridge had an unmarked switch inside. When she saw I had flipped it a few times, my sister told me that the switch turned the neighbors' house upside down. I believed her until I was about five, at which point I flipped it, ran outside, and was very relieved to find their house right-side up.

Dave

When I was a little girl
I really wanted pierced ears
and thought that when you
reached a certain age, the little
holes grew by themselves.

Kate

My granny always told me that I
would grow horns if I lay down while
I was eating. When she wasn't looking,
I would lie down and chew my food,
feeling for the horns on my head.

Megan

It took me a long time to realize that "gorilla cheese sandwiches" were actually *grilled*-cheese sandwiches and were not prepared by, with, or for a gorilla.

Suzy

I thought that countries really
had their names written across
them, like they do on maps, and
that at the borders there were
red dotted lines on the ground.

Looby

I used to think that I could be anything I wanted when I grew up. I wanted to be an airport, and my best friend wanted to be a fire truck.

B.

Since both my parents had the same last name, I thought you had to marry someone with your last name. I didn't want to marry the only girl I knew with my same last name, so in 4th grade I bit her on the arm.

Anonymous

After my grandfather died
I thought he was in my closet,
hanging up behind my coat.

Jim

I thought kosher foods were on
the anim

here the rabbi took
to the house and read to it.

As a child I would sing along with
the Beatles' "Eight Days a Week."
For years afterward I thought I
was miscounting, because I couldn't
name the eighth day.   *Eric*

When we were very young, my sister
and I would avoid the dining room.
We thought that since there was a
living room, the dining room was the
dying room, where people went to die.

Miss Chockie

At our school everyone was given a chicken drumstick for Christmas lunch. I remember thinking that it was a terrible waste of the rest of the chicken.

Debbie

I thought that **birds** grew

from birdseed.

Jen

I used to think that everyone except me
was a robot. I abandoned this theory when
my friend asked me if I was a robot.

Will

When we were young, my brother and I decided that the vacuum cleaner must get terribly thirsty because of all the dust it picked up. We sucked up a soda to quench its thirst. Our mom wasn't pleased the next time she tried to use it.

Lau

I thought that a birthmark was a *birdmark,* and that if bird poo landed on you when you were a baby, it stained your skin and wouldn't wash off.

Anonymous

When I was really little
I believed that if the car's
hazard warning lights
came on, the car would
split in half: one half would
turn left and the other
right. Needless to say,
I was terrified of sitting
in the middle.

Anghi

My mom used to tell me that there was a banana factory
where bananas were bent before they were sold.

H.

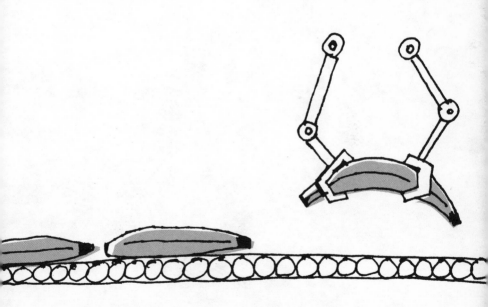

I used to believe that porcupines wer

humongous

pine trees that could hurt you.

Shelly

I believed that the holes

in Swiss cheese were

cow farts.

Lily

I was told that diamonds
were made out of coal crushed
under the earth, so I put a piece
of coal under a brick in the
garden and checked it regularly.
I knew I didn't have enough
pressure for a diamond, but I
figured I'd get something good—
possibly chocolate.

Chris

When my dad said that kids were being brainwashed,
I thought that meant that people literally opened up
your head and washed your brain with soap and water.

Carlos

I used to believe that boogers were little bugs that went up your nose and died when you were asleep, and then they dried up and you had to pick them out in the morning when you woke up.

F.

I used to think that Napoleon invented Neapolitan ice cream.

Anonymous

I believed that wildflowers really were wild. I was terrified at the thought of going into the country-side, in case I was attacked by some.

Peter

We used to tell my younger brother that if you ate watermelon seeds, a watermelon would grow in your stomach. So he decided that to grow a baby, you had to eat baby seeds.

Anonymous

I thought that cologne would make me smell better if I drank it.

D.

One time when I was little I was walking with my mom and we came to the edge of a very steep hill. As I set off gleefully down the slope she called, "Be careful! Don't run too fast or you won't be able to stop." After this I thought that once people ran faster than a certain speed they would be doomed to run everywhere for the rest of their lives.

Jo

Visiting the public library as a kid, I assumed that most of the books in the grown-up section were filled with pictures of people "doing it."

T.

When I was four or five, my parents grounded me for the first time. I told my friends through the screen door that I'd never see them again, because I thought my parents were going to bury me up to my neck in the backyard.

e.

I thought that a cat
burglar was either a
burglar who stole cats
or some kind of evil,
burgling cat.

Anonymous

When I was four, I believed that if you scrubbed a vinyl record hard enough, you could erase it and record your own songs on it.

Dave

I used to believe that to quit a bad habit all you needed to do was eat some cold turkey.

Randy

At church, my mom used to throw leftover quarters from the past week into the collection basket. I thought the priest used them to play video games at the arcade.

S.

I used
to think
sheep

shrank

when it
rained.

Anonymous

When I was around five, I would lie on the floor next to the air conditioning vent. I thought that all the vents in the world were connected, and I would yell into mine, hoping that another kid had figured it out too so we could talk to each other.

Christopher

A friend at school said that when you sneeze, you actually die for a split second. *Alex*

I thought that the hazard warning button in cars would get you out of trouble. For instance, if your car got stuck, you could press the hazard button and the car would sprout massive legs with suction cups on the end and walk away.

Lukas

I used to believe
that the loser
of the presidential
election became
the vice president.

A.

I used to believe that some puddles
didn't have bottoms, and if you jumped
into them, you'd fall forever and ever.

Abi

As a seven-year-old Irish Catholic I was used to hearing the Hail Mary, but the line "blessed art thou amongst women" sounded like "blessed art thou, *a monk swimming.*"

John

When I was eight my older brother told me that because of the spin of the earth, if anyone faced exactly east, they would fly off into space. I'd never heard of this, so when I questioned it he said that very few people had ever actually done it because it was almost impossible.

John

I was three when my mother taught me the song "Silent Night," with the line "Sleep in heavenly peace." I thought that when you went to heaven, you slept on a bed of peas, and if you got hungry, you could eat them. Peas were my favorite vegetable, so heaven sounded really good.

Gigi

I used to believe that Bo and Luke Duke (from the TV show *The Dukes of Hazzard*) could see me through the television. I had a huge crush on Bo and would fluff my hair, put on my best nightie, and smile at him throughout the program.   *Alex*

I thought that the reflectors in the road were to alert blind people when they changed lanes. *Nonny*

When I saw ads for toys that said "batteries not included," I thought it meant that the toy didn't need batteries to work. When I asked my parents for a toy, I would add "batteries not included" as a selling point, because I thought they'd be happy they wouldn't have to buy batteries.

Anonymous

I thought that birds had special shoes from the electricity

...oots to protect them
...hen they stood on high wires.

I used to believe that going gray was a warning that the hair in your head was running out, like a roll of tape in a cash register turning a different color to let you know it's nearly gone.

Fiona

I believed that when a cat ate a mouse, the mouse went to
live in the cat's tail: cats' tails appeared to move independent
of the rest of the cat, and this would explain why

cats liked to chase their tails.

Ness

At age seven I saw a show about atomic bombs that mentioned the destructive force caused by splitting atoms. After that I thought there was a chance that I could split an atom while cutting bread with a knife. I was terrified that by cutting my jelly sandwich I might accidentally wipe my town off the map.

S.

When I was young I used to believe that a walk-in closet
was one that could bring your clothes to you.

Anonymous

Whenever my mom
cooked a chicken,

my brother and I used
to fight over the legs, so
she would always buy
an extra pack of legs.
She and my brother had
me convinced that they
had come from a six-
legged racing chicken.

S.

I used to believe that all babies are born as girls, and if you sneeze or cough too hard, you become a boy. I dreaded having a cold, and when I sneezed I would rush to the bathroom just to make sure I hadn't "popped."

Lucy

I was horrified when my first period arrived: it wasn't **blue** like in the commercials for sanitary napkins.

Jane

When I saw headlines on TV like "Bank robbery, two people killed, news at **11:00**," I thought that they knew it was going to happen at eleven o'clock and wondered why they didn't stop it beforehand.

Anonymous

The first time we took our cat to the vet, I was
shocked to find out that the veterinarian was human.
I'd always pictured a dog in a white lab coat.

Patty

When I was a kid, I thought that toothpaste was made from teeth. It made sense: tomato paste is made from tomatoes.

Andy

I had a pad of multicolored construction paper and was convinced that each color was a flavor, like blueberry, strawberry, or grape. I ate little pieces of the paper and was certain that I could detect the subtle nuances of flavor in each one.

J.

I used to believe that armadillos only lived in Amarillo.

Laura

I thought that being sentenced to death meant that you'd have to write the same sentence over and over again until you died.

Anonymous

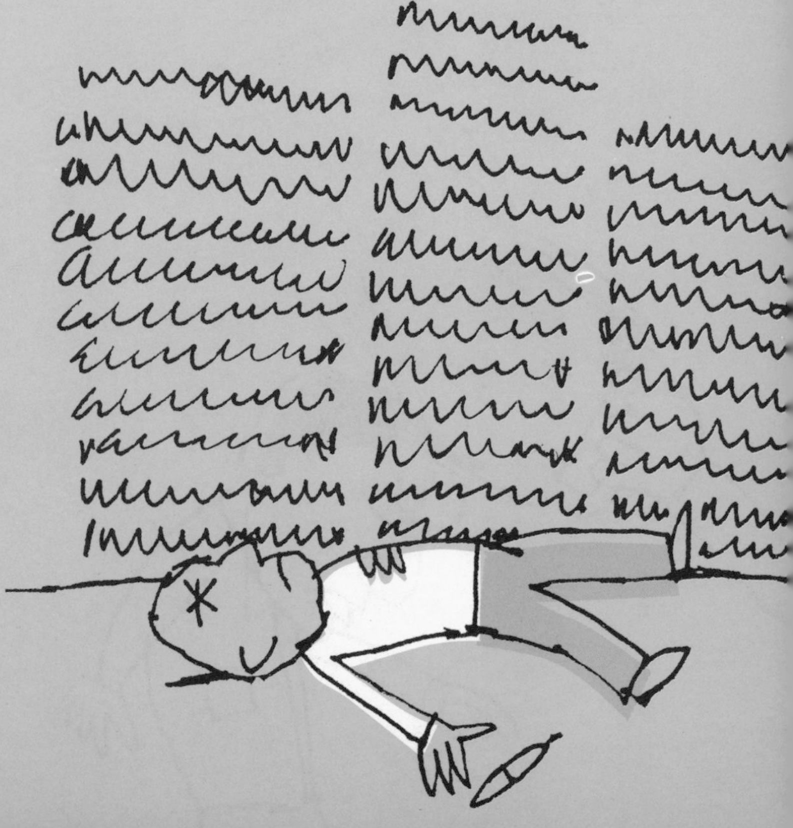

I used to believe that "being mugged"
meant that someone hit you with a coffee mug.

Matt T.

I remember learning that when police officers read people their rights, they say that anything "can and will be used against you in a court of law." I thought that if you said "Crabs" or "Alligators" or "Spiders," they could be used to torture you on the witness stand.

Amanda

When I was a kid I overheard my parents talking about the baby boom. I thought it was a problem of small children suddenly exploding. *Alan*

When I was younger, my parents told me that if I peed in the pool, it would rise to the top and spell out my name. *Ashley*

I used to believe that weather forecasters decided what the weather would be. When they forecasted rain for my area, I thought they were deliberately being mean.

Michael A.

My brother told me that I was so ugly my parents had to pay people to stand behind mirrors and pretend to be me, so that I wouldn't know the truth. He said that this was why our family was poor.

S.

When I was five, I attended a Catholic
school in New York where the nuns wore
long black habits. They seemed to glide
around the classroom and you could never
see their feet, so I believed that God had
given the nuns wheels instead of feet.

Diane

I thought that
Napoleon invented
linoleum.

Steve M.

My older sisters told me that electricity was in the ground, so I used to go around plugging radios and all sorts of stuff into the ground. To my surprise, they never worked.

John P.

I wanted to be a con artist when I grew up and planned to go to college to learn the trade.

R.P.

8

Did anyone else sing, "Hark, the hairy angels sing"?

Jill

When I was young,
I used to believe
that R.I.P. meant
"Return if Possible."

Colin

I thought that my backside was perfectly round until my mom smacked me one day and I noticed in the bathroom mirror for the very first time that my bottom had a crack. I told her that she'd broken it!   *Mark*

I believed that if you tried to smoke under the legal age, the cigarette would know and explode.
                    Anonymous

My cousin and I were curious
about the phrase

> "The wind will change and your
> face will stay like that."

She used to pull stupid faces and
I would blow on her face slowly and then
quickly, as if the wind really were chang-
ing, in the hope of seeing her face get
stuck like that.

Daria

9

We used to drive along a road with big, overhanging trees, one of which had a BEWARE OF PEDESTRIANS sign on it. We told our little brother that pedestrians were like octopuses that dropped down on cars from the trees and ate everybody inside. He believed this for years.

J.

My grandfather lost a thumb in an
accident at work. Although we were
very close, I never noticed this until
I was five years old, while watching
him use a typewriter one day. The very
next day I discovered he had removable
dentures. After that I thought that
it was a normal part of becoming an
adult for your body parts to be replaced
by larger, detachable ones.

Carson

At age seven I thought
that if I looked at a map
closely enough, I would
be able to see people
running around.

Adam

I used to believe that when you died you turned into an animal, so when I got a dog, I named it Granny.

Bob

I didn't understand how medicine knew where your body hurt. How did it know whether you had toothache or a tummy ache? I thought my mom gave it directions as she poured it onto the spoon.

Molly

I believed that steel woo

came from steel sheep.

T.G.

I thought that when you died
your coffin was taken up to heaven
by helicopter. I wanted to be
buried in the cupboard from my
old school room, because the doors
didn't quite shut properly and I
would be able to take advantage
of the great views.

Jo

I was with my dad in the car one day when he threw an apple core out the window. Thinking this was cool, I threw my packet of chips out the window as well. Dad told me I shouldn't litter, but when I told him I'd just seen him do it, he said, "It's different; an apple is biodegradable." For years afterward I thought biodegradable meant something adults were allowed to do that kids weren't.

Pat

I thought everything had feelings: furniture, bugs, pens, you name it. Getting ice was the worst. When I took ice out of the freezer I tried to leave a few cubes near one another so that they wouldn't get lonely. Then I started wondering, What if the ice cubes I left near one another didn't get along? So then I had to consider whether it was better for an ice cube to be lonely or have to put up with unfriendly cubes.

Sampa

The first time I phoned a company's customer service, they put me on hold and some music started playing. I thought that the operator had got out her recorder and was playing it for me over the phone.

Helen

I thought I had a family of frogs in my belly. I think this belief came from the expression "a frog in your throat," but I thought they had moved down to live in my tummy. *Kirk*

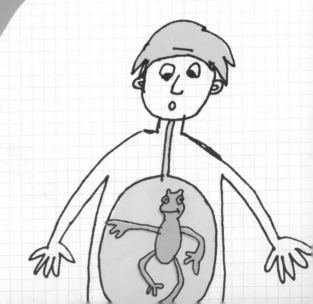

When I was little I was terrified
of fiberglass insulation. I thought
that if I got too close, it would
reach out from the walls, suck
me in, and eat me alive.

Heather

I asked my older brother where store man-
nequins came from, and he told me that the
store manager had shot a ray at shoplifters
and turned them into stone. That is why
they were in such odd poses: because they
were desperately running away when the
ray got them. I was afraid that I would see
a mannequin I recognized someday.

Pat

When I was little, I used to believe that if you put your hands in the air, you couldn't be killed. That was the reason why everybody in *Starsky and Hutch* put their hands up whenever anyone pulled a gun.

Andy

If I was wet and walked past something that smelled very bad, I worried that the smell would stick to me.

Jill

I used to believe that the black market was a real flea market somewhere in Central America where you could buy stolen paintings and Russian tanks.

Shannon

When I was younger I was scared to get out
of bed during the night because I thought that
gravity turned off when the sun went down
and I would just float away.

Lindsey

I once asked my mom what the little specks flying around in the sunshine were. She said they were flying dust, but I misunderstood and thought she had said flying *dogs*.

Liz

I thought that the term *prima donna* was actually *pre-Madonna,* referring to a singer who made pop music in the style that was common before Madonna became popular (cf. *pre-Raphaelite*).

Ollie

My friend Sergio told me he thought that the slicks of oil in puddles were dead rainbows.

Allen

My dad was in the navy when I was young and was away quite a lot. My sister and I wrote letters to him, and my mom would take us to the mailbox. My sister thought he lived inside it and shouted things to him through the slot.

Katy

I believed that I had an endless supply of teeth that would fall out and grow back for the rest of my life.

Klayne

Somebody told me that they cut down rain forests to make McDonald's hamburgers, so for years I thought that burgers were made of wood.   *Anonymous*

One day my little sister received a rather nasty gash above the eye (my fault) and was taken to hospital. Waiting outside, I wondered how the doctor would fit my sister's head under the sewing machine to do the stitches.

F.

I used to think that the cold war took place in Siberia or Alaska.

Liam

I was told that you had to hold your breath
while passing a graveyard, otherwise you'd
get cemetery breath and die within a few days.
There was a huge cemetery near my house,
but my family never noticed me turning blue
each time we drove past it.

Chris

I used to think that if you
shined a flashlight into the
sky at night, an airplane
would think you were a
runway and land on you.

S.

As a four-year-old
I thought a civil war
was where everybody
pretended to be nice.

Hannah

My dad was in the navy, and every other Friday he had to take his sword to work. My brother thought that on those days he was on pirate-fighting duty

Colin

I thought that when mice died they became bats.

Julio

One day at school we killed a huge spider, making green-and-white fluid come out. For quite a while I believed that spiders were filled with toothpaste.

Anonymous

I thought that if I let my cat, Rusty, sleep on my bed with me, I would get pregnant and have kittens, and my mom would be really mad at me.

Rachel

After learning that everyone
has a soul, I wondered where
it was located. Every body
part seemed to be occupied,
and I finally concluded that
the chin was the only part
without a function, so the
soul had to be housed there.

Darlene

I used to think that when people said their leg had fallen asleep, it meant that their leg was resting. When mine fell asleep, I would try not to disturb it.

Tiff

Someone told me that if I turned my head really fast, I could bite my own ear. I tried it and almost ended up with whiplash. My grandma said that if I kissed my own elbow, I would be able to fly.   *Kitty*

I thought eyes were made of water, and if you opened them underwater, they would dissolve and come out of your head.

Joel

I used to believe that
mustaches were just long,
flowing nose hair.

 A.

Ooooh

Ooooh

I used to think that our house was haunted. When I had to get up in the middle of the night I would drape a blanket over my head and shuffle toward the bathroom, "Ooo-ing" softly, so that any passing ghosts would think I was one of them.

K.

I thought that if you shouted into a balloon while you were blowing it up, the same noise would come out when you popped it. *James*

My daughter once asked if
God was short for *Godfrey.*

K.

Whenever TV broadcasters had problems, a standard message would appear saying, "Technical difficulties, please stand by." I thought that meant I had to go and stand by the TV.

Jansam

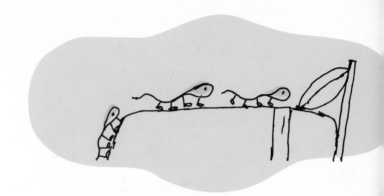

When I was about eight or nine, my father sat me down and told me the facts of life. He explained how a man and a woman got in bed together and sperm from the man would fertilize the woman's egg. I used to climb into bed with my parents and look under the bedclothes to see if I could see any sperm moving like a trail of ants from one side of the bed to the other.

Anonymous

When I was drawing a
map I thought I had to
be really careful, because
if I got it wrong it would
change the real coastline.

Claire

I won a goldfish at the fair that died after a couple of weeks. So my parents and I flushed it down the toilet, and after that I thought you could flush away any pets you didn't want anymore. My grandmother had a little black poodle that I hated, so once when I was at her house I tried to flush it down the toilet.

Debs

I used to believe that if you saved the crud that collects in your eyes overnight, it would eventually grow into a whole new eyeball.

Anonymous

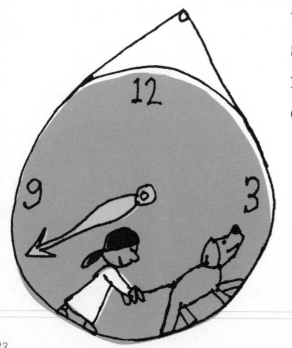

I thought that if I didn't take my dog for lots of walks she would explode, so I walked my dog every other hour.

Lucy B.

I thought that the
Godzilla movies were
documentaries and
felt sorry for people
in Japan who kept
getting attacked.

Niki

When I was three, I knew that brains
made you smart, but I did not know
what they were. I thought they might
be special strands of hair and was afraid
to have my hair cut, because I did not
want my brains cut short.

Shedona

When I watched horror movies as a kid, my stomach would become very knotted. I thought that this was because it was watching the movie, too, so I would stand behind a chair to shield my stomach from the scary scenes.

𝒦.

I believed that the credits at the end of a movie were a list of the people who were watching it.

Jon

When I first heard the expression "post nasal-drip," I thought it was a cereal.

Nancy

I used to wonder how people knew which side of the street to drive on. I decided that who-ever got up first picked the side of the street for the rest of the day.

Anonymous

When I was a little kid, my older sister told me that sometimes the Tooth Fairy got drunk and took an eye by mistake.

Derek

When she was a child, a friend's aunt didn't
understand why, during mass, she had to sing
about a cross-eyed bear called Gladly. Years
later she found out that she was supposed
to be ready to support Jesus by confirming
"gladly, the cross I'd bear."

Jankai

I used to believe that there were hundreds of mechanical chickens hiding in my closet. When the wind made the door bump, I was sure it was the chicken army trying to escape. I wasn't sure what an army of mechanical chickens would actually do, but it was scary.

P.

When I was about six or seven, I believed that a little penguin lived in my refrigerator and turned the interior light on and off. I opened the fridge repeatedly, trying to catch him in the act.

Bee

When I was very young a friend of my mother's whose leg had been amputated would come to visit. When she drank coffee I waited with great anticipation, thinking that it would drip out.

Alicia

When I was 4 or 5, I believed that the candy bar called "100 Grand," actually cost $100,000! I never tried to buy it because I only had 50 cents or so in my pocket.

S.

I thought that your bottom teeth were in your bottom.

Jez

I used to think that I could control the weather, and when I was nine I said that I wanted snow for Christmas. We got so much snow that year that everyone was trapped in their homes, and I swore never to use my powers again.

Mel

In kindergarten I thought that when reading, you read the page and then turned the book around and waved the page back and forth. Little did I know the teacher was just showing us the pictures and that was not required if you were reading to yourself.

Ryan

My mother once told me that you had to go to a special school to learn how to be a criminal. I imagined kids sitting at desks learning how to rob and getting homework assignments to go and kill someone.

W.

When I was four, my sister told me the "truth": that my real parents were rabbits and my dad had discovered me in the backyard while mowing the lawn. She said mom and dad took me in because they felt bad about almost running me over with the lawn mower. For years afterward I'd see a rabbit and wonder if it was a relative.

Bing

My older sister got a lift to
school each day in a car pool.
I couldn't wait to start school,
because I thought it was a
swimming pool on wheels.

Jan

I used to believe that someone
with a "sweet tooth" actually had
a tooth that tasted like candy.
I was disappionted to find that
I didn't have a sweet tooth.

Kit

My older brother told me
that if you ate nothing but
bananas and Vaseline, you
would live forever.   *P.*

I thought ladies
with big **bouffant**
hairdos had heads
shaped that way.

Bea

I read that you can see ghosts
only in mirrors, but you can't
see vampires in them at all. This
made looking in the mirror very
tricky, because I'd have to check
for ghosts and then whip my
head around every few seconds
to make sure no vampires were
sneaking up on me.

Cris

When I was
little I was
absolutely
positive that
butter was
made by
butterflies

Ruth

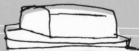

I used to open all the drawers in our house so that the things inside them could breathe properly.

Anonymous

I used to believe that the ridges on the roof of my mouth spelled out *Made in Japan,* like on the bottom of my doll's foot.

Karen

Until I was about ten,
I thought that my
parents transformed
into enormous ants when
I couldn't see them.

Maja

My brother told me that the pieces of peel in orange marmalade were the chopped-up remains of Fred and Freda, my dead goldfish. Twenty years later, I still won't eat marmalade.

K.

I was a child during the Cuban Missile Crisis, and I used to believe that when schoolteachers went to their break room they worked on rockets to fight the Soviets and Cubans.

Hollis

I believed that macaroni was made from crows' knees.

Jason

I used to believe that we had invisible giraffes
in our house. Whenever my mother said,

"There's a draft in here,"

I used to think that she was saying "giraffe."
The idea of something that large wandering
around the house without me being able to
see it was quite frightening.   *Penny*

I thought my teachers secretly lived at school over the summer, in big pickle jars full of some kind of fluid and maybe plugged into electric outlets to recharge.

Tiff

When the toaster popped up my toast in the morning, my daughter used to call, "Dad, your toast is here!" She thought it was delivered each morning through the toaster.

Mark

My dad used to take my brother and me mush-
room hunting. We had to leave early so that the
mushrooms would still be asleep, then creep up
the field slowly and throw our coats over them
before they ran away.

G.

Although I grew up near Chicago, with no mountains in sight, I always wanted the top bunk so that if a volcano erupted nearby, I would be safe from flowing lava.

Frannie

When I was in kindergarten
a little boy threw a worm
into my hair, and for years
I believed that people
carried umbrellas because
worms fell from the sky.

Laura

Because my name is Elizabeth, I thought that I would be the next queen of England, and that I lived with my family only because the royal family wanted me to have a proper upbringing.

Elizabeth

As a child
I thought that
if I jumped
too high on
my trampoline,
I'd get sucked
into space.

Jenn

I used to believe that the number of peopl
fingers you had

I had a strange fear that if I
closed my eyes in the bathtub,
William Shakespeare would
come up through the drain and
kill me. I knew his name but
had no idea who he was, so I
naturally assumed he was some
sort of bathtub vampire.

Dan

n your family dictated how many
ince there were five of us, I had five fingers.

Evelyn

I used to think there was a place called Gunpoint and could never understand why people still went there.

Elizabeth

I used to believe that airline pilots drove really fast down the runways just to show off.

Anonymous

I believed that checks were free money, and that if you wrote one for $1,000,000, you would have a million dollars. When I asked my mom to buy me toys and she said they cost too much, I told her to write a check. *Marsh*

I thought that candle wax came from dead people's ears, because someone told me it was a man-made substance.

David

As a very young child I thought that the army, air force, and navy all fought one another for a living. While visiting an air force base, I was shocked to see a woman wearing fatigues. I assumed she was in the army, and I expected some of the airmen to attack her.

Jon

When I was four, I thought that you could dig a hole to China. My mother found me in the backyard, trowel in one hand and a suitcase in the other, and asked me what I was doing. I informed her that I was going to China for the week and would be back in time for church.

J.

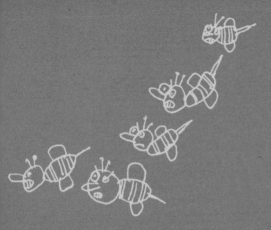

I didn't understand why the British national anthem was called "God Save the Queen" and asked my brother why she needed saving. He said that she was being chased by swarms of bees.

Anonymous

When I was a little kid I thought that if you gave somebody your cold, you would no longer be sick. When I had one, I would kiss people and then breathe two short breaths in their face to give it to them. *R.*

I used to believe that my marbles were tiny planets. I thought that if I kept them in the dark for too long, the inhabitants would die, so for years I'd get my marbles out every morning and put them back into their box every night. I even took my box on holidays with me. *Lassy*

I used to believe that pigs laid sausages.

Stuart

My parents used to tell me that I should wear clean underwear every day in case I was in a car accident. I grew up thinking that my underwear could stop traffic.

Anonymous

My friend Peggy told me that if you stared at the sun long enough you would go blonde.

Suzy

I used to think that after signing an organ donor card someone came to take your organs out straight away. My mum filled one in and I got really upset and tore it up.

A.

When I was little I firmly believed that my stuffed animals were alive, and I would burst into my bedroom, trying to catch them in the act of talking or moving. I didn't give my toys names, because they already had their own names—I just didn't know what they were, because they never spoke when I was around.

Rita

When I was three, my parents told me that carrots help you see in the dark. That night they found me trying to use a carrot as a flashlight.

Emma

My dad told me that the big bales
of hay I saw wrapped in plastic in
farmers' fields were cow eggs.

Anonymous

I used to be convinced
that all my grandmother
did between our visits
was stand at her door
waving, since it was the
last thing she did when
we left and the first thing
she did when we arrived.
Sometimes I wouldn't
see her for weeks and
would worry that she
must be exhausted.

I used to think that eyelash curlers were eyeball removers. I thought it was gross but cool that people could change the color of their eyes by switching eyeballs whenever they wanted.

M.

I thought that the gas tank in our car worked like a timer, so that if the tank was almost empty, you just had to drive faster to get to the service station before the gas ran out. I used to suggest this solution to my parents every time they said we needed gas.

Alyson

the end